First Facts®

SCIENCE **BASICS**

WHAT IS SOUND?

by Jody S. Rake

raintree
a Capstone company—publishers for children
www.raintree.co.uk

Raintree is an imprint of Capstone Global Library Limited, a company incorporated in England and Wales having its registered office at 264 Banbury Road, Oxford, OX2 7DY – Registered company number: 6695582

www.raintree.co.uk
myorders@raintree.co.uk

Edited by Jaclyn Jaycox and Mari Bolte
Designed by Kyle Grentz
Original illustrations © Capstone Global Library Limited 2019
Picture research by Eric Gohl
Production by Laura Manthe
Originated by Capstone Global Library Ltd
Printed and bound in India

ISBN 978 1 4747 7084 2
23 22 21 20 19
10 9 8 7 6 5 4 3 2 1

British Library Cataloguing in Publication Data
A full catalogue record for this book is available from the British Library.

Acknowledgements
We would like to thank the following for permission to reproduce photographs: Capstone Studio: Karon Dubke, 20–21; Shutterstock: Anton Havelaar, 9 (bottom right), Daxiao Productions, 15, deedeenaja, 7, EarnestTse, 5, f11photo, cover, ilusmedical, 13, India Picture, 9 (bottom left), inspiron.dell.vector, 19 (cell phone & tower), Jemastock, 19 (satellite), Litvalifa, 9 (top), Mike Monahan, 19, Roman Voloshyn, 17 (back), saicle, background (throughout), Sermchai PurnPorn, 8, Trofimov Denis, 17 (inset).

Every effort has been made to contact copyright holders of material reproduced in this book. Any omissions will be rectified in subsequent printings if notice is given to the publisher.

All the internet addresses (URLs) given in this book were valid at the time of going to press. However, due to the dynamic nature of the internet, some addresses may have changed, or sites may have changed or ceased to exist since publication. While the author and publisher regret any inconvenience this may cause readers, no responsibility for any such changes can be accepted by either the author or the publisher.

CONTENTS

SOUNDS
ALL AROUND

Birds chirping, music playing, friends laughing. Every minute of the day you hear sounds.

Sound happens when an object **vibrates**. The vibration pushes on groups of atoms called air **molecules**. These molecules bump into other molecules. This action is called a sound **wave**. The sound wave travels through the air to your ears.

vibrate move back and forth quickly
molecule atoms making up the smallest unit of a substance
wave energy usually moving through air or water

FACT

Sound waves travel 343 metres (1,125 feet) per second. That is almost the length of four football pitches!

SOUND
IS A **WAVE**

Sound waves travel in all directions. If you throw a stone into a still pond, it makes ripples. The ripples move out in growing circles. The circles then start to fade. Sound waves work like this in air. The further you are from the sound, the weaker the waves are.

LOUD AND SOFT, HIGH AND LOW

Different sounds are caused by different sound waves. Louder sounds create larger sound waves. Quieter sounds create smaller sound waves.

Sound waves determine a sound's **pitch**. Higher-pitched sounds have a higher **frequency**. This means they vibrate many times each second. Lower sounds vibrate more slowly.

pitch how high or low a sound is
frequency number of sound waves that pass a location in a certain amount of time

Loud

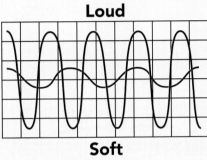

Soft

Low Frequency

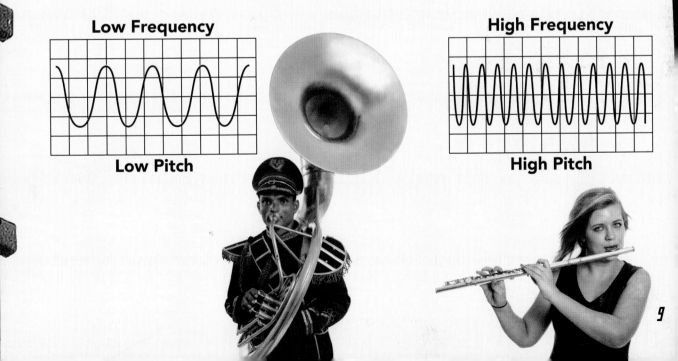

Low Pitch

High Frequency

High Pitch

9

SOUND THROUGH
AIR, LIQUIDS AND SOLIDS

Sounds can travel through more than just air. They can go through liquids and solids too. Molecules in liquid are closer together than they are in air. This allows sound waves to travel faster and further in liquid. Molecules in solids are even closer together than in liquids.

OCEAN ECHOES

Dolphins use sound to communicate with each other. They also use sound to help them learn. This special type of sound is called echolocation. A dolphin sends high-pitched whistles out into the water. The sound waves bounce off objects. They echo back to the dolphin. This lets the dolphin "see" objects. The echo tells them how far away and how big the objects are.

SOLID

LIQUID

GAS

RECEIVING SOUND: HOW EARS WORK

Our ears are designed to receive sounds. Sound waves reach the eardrum and tiny bones, causing them to vibrate. The bones carry the vibrations to the **cochlea**. The cochlea is in the inner ear. It contains thousands of very tiny hairs. Different sounds make different hairs vibrate. **Nerves** attached to the cochlea pick up the sound. The nerves then carry the sound message to the brain.

cochlea spiral-shaped part of the ear that helps send sound messages to the brain
nerve thin fibre that carries messages between the brain and other parts of the body

DIAGRAM OF AN EAR

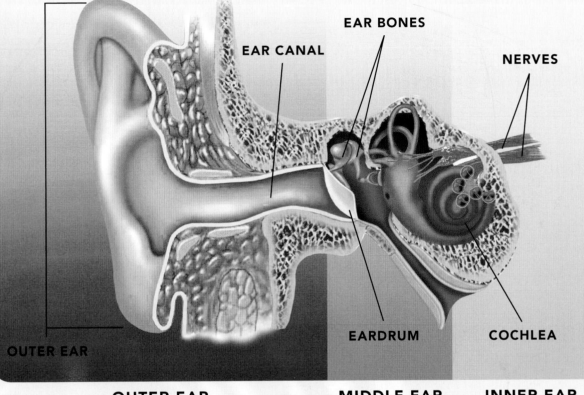

EAR BONES

EAR CANAL

NERVES

OUTER EAR

EARDRUM

COCHLEA

OUTER EAR   MIDDLE EAR   INNER EAR

People who have trouble hearing often use hearing aids. These small objects fit inside the ear. They use a tiny microphone called an **amplifier** to make sounds louder.

amplifier piece of equipment that makes sound louder

SOUNDS FOR
COMMUNICATION

Sound is an important part of communication. Animals and humans make sounds to communicate with each other. A baby's cry tells its mother that it is hungry. Sounds can also give us information and warn us of danger. A school bell tells us it's time for break. A fire alarm warns us to get to safety.

15

SOUNDS
AND MUSIC

Musical instruments make sounds in different ways. Stringed instruments work when you pluck or rub the strings. Different lengths of strings make different pitches. Woodwind and brass instruments work when you blow air through a tube. You hear high or low sounds by controlling the opening in the tube. **Percussion** instruments make sound when you strike them. You hear different sounds based on the instrument's size, shape and material.

percussion instruments that create sound when they are struck or shaken

FACT

Acoustic guitars have hollow wooden bodies. The air space inside the guitar makes its music louder. Electric guitars usually do not have hollow bodies. They use electric amplifiers to make sound louder.

acoustic music not enhanced by an amplifier

HOW
PHONES WORK

When you speak into a phone, a microphone turns your voice into an electrical signal. The signal from a wired telephone travels through wires. A mobile phone signal travels through the air. The signal is then turned back into sound by the other person's phone.

TURNING SOUND INTO TEXT

Computers can turn the sound of your voice into text on a screen. A microphone receives vibrations made by your voice. It turns the vibrations into small sounds a computer can understand. The computer compares these sounds to a huge library of words in its memory. Then it turns the information to text.

Mobile phone signals travel to towers. Some mobile towers send the signals to a **satellite** in space. The satellite bounces the signals back to other mobile towers. This whole trip takes less than one second!

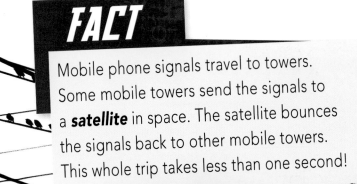

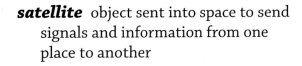

satellite object sent into space to send signals and information from one place to another

SOUND EXPERIMENT

MATERIALS:

- clingfilm
- medium glass bowl
- 1 teaspoon (5 millilitres) cornflour
- 1 teaspoon water
- small glass bowl
- spoon

WHAT TO DO:

1. Stretch clingfilm across the top of the medium bowl and seal it tightly. Make sure there are no wrinkles.

2. Mix the cornflour and water in the small bowl with a spoon until smooth.

3. Scoop a small amount of the cornflour mixture over the clingfilm. It should be close to the middle. If there are any bubbles, lightly touch them with your fingertip to pop them.

4. Get your face very close to the bowl. Hum loudly. Can you see anything happen to the cornflour mixture?

5. Gently touch your fingertips to the clingfilm and hum again. Can you feel anything?

SOUND TRAVELLING THROUGH A SOLID

MATERIALS:

- metal fork
- wooden table
- watch or timer
- a friend

WHAT TO DO:

1. Holding the fork loosely by the end of the handle, strike the tines (pointed end) on the table. What can you hear? How long does the sound last? Repeat this step and time the sound with your timer.

2. Put your head down on one end of the table with your ear touching the surface. Ask your friend to strike the fork on the other end. Then immediately touch the tip of the handle to the tabletop. What can you hear? How long does it last? Repeat this step using your timer.

3. You can also experiment with different types of surfaces (metal, plastic, glass or stone). Which surface does sound travel through the best?

GLOSSARY

acoustic sound not enhanced by an amplifier

amplifier machine that makes sounds louder

cochlea part of the ear that helps send sound messages to the brain

frequency number of sound waves that pass a location in a certain amount of time

molecules atoms making up the smallest unit of a substance; H_2O is a molecule of water

nerve thin fibre that carries messages between the brain and other parts of the body

percussion instruments that create sound when they are struck or shaken

pitch how high or low a sound is

satellite object sent into space to send signals and information from one place to another

vibrate move back and forth quickly

wave energy usually moving through air or water

FIND OUT MORE

BOOKS

Sound (Young Explorer: All About Science), Angela Royston (Raintree, 2017)

The Sounds Around Us (Engage Literacy), Kelly Gaffney (Raintree, 2017)

Why Can't I Hear That?: Pitch and Frequency (Exploring Sound), Louise and Richard Spilsbury (Raintree, 2015)

WEBSITES

www.bbc.co.uk/guides/z3j3jty
Learn more about pitch!

www.dkfindout.com/uk/science/sound/how-are-sounds-created
Find out more about how sounds are created.